THE PARADOX OF ROBERT OPPENHEIMER

From Quantum Mechanics to the Atomic Bomb: A Journey Through the Manhattan Project and Beyond

ALBERT NEUTRON

Copyright © 2023 Albert Neutron

All rights reserved. No part of this publication may be reproduced, distributed or transmitted in any form or by any means, including photocopying, recording, or other electronic or mechanical methods, without the prior written permission of the publisher, except in the case of brief quotations embodied in critical reviews and certain other non-commercial uses permitted by copyright law.

Trademarked names appear throughout this book. Rather than use a trademark symbol with every occurrence of a trademarked name, names are used in an editorial fashion, with no intention of infringement of the respective owner's trademark. The information in this book is distributed on an "as is" basis, without warranty. Although every precaution has been taken in the preparation of this work, neither the author nor the publisher shall have any liability to any person or entity with respect to any loss or damage caused or alleged to be caused directly or indirectly by the information contained in this book.

"We knew the world would not be the same. A few people laughed, a few people cried. Most people were silent. I remembered the line from the Hindu scripture, the Bhagavad-Gita; Vishnu is trying to persuade the Prince that he should do his duty, and to impress him, takes on his multi-armed form and says, 'Now I am become Death, the destroyer of worlds.' I suppose we all thought that, one way or another."

- J. Robert Oppenheimer

Contents

1. The Enigma of Oppenheimer — 1
2. The Early Years: Birth to College — 5
3. The Quantum Mechanic: Oppenheimer's Academic Journey — 11
4. The Berkeley Years: Teaching and Research — 19
5. The Political Awakening: Oppenheimer's Ideological Shift — 29
6. The Manhattan Project: The Birth of the Atomic Bomb — 39
7. The Trinity Test and the Culmination of the Manhattan Project — 51
8. Reflections: The Ambivalence of the Atomic Architect — 59
9. Later Life and Career — 69
10. The Red Scare and Oppenheimer's Fall from Grace — 75
11. The Scientist, Philosopher and Statesman — 81
12. Resolving Oppenheimer's Paradox — 87

ONE

The Enigma of Oppenheimer

In the annals of history, few figures are as enigmatic and compelling as Julius Robert Oppenheimer. A man of profound intellect and equally profound contradictions, Oppenheimer stands as a testament to the paradoxical nature of genius. He was a physicist, a philosopher, a lover of literature, and the father of the atomic bomb. His life was a tapestry of triumphs and tragedies, woven together by the threads of his insatiable curiosity and his relentless pursuit of knowledge.

Oppenheimer was a man who straddled two worlds. In one, he was a scientist, a seeker of truth in the realm of the physical universe. On the other, he was a humanist, a man deeply concerned with the moral and ethical implications of the very truths he sought. This duality is what makes Oppenheimer such a fascinating figure. He was not just a scientist, but a man of deep philosophical insight. He was not just a creator of weapons of mass destruction, but a man who agonized over their use.

This book aims to unravel the enigma that is Julius Robert Oppenheimer. It seeks to delve into the depths of his mind, explore the forces that shaped him, and understand the impact he had on the world. It is a journey into the heart of a man who, in many ways, is a mirror of the twentieth century itself - a time of unprecedented scientific advancement and equally unprecedented human suffering.

The story of Oppenheimer is not just the story of a man, but the story of an era. It is a tale of ambition and hubris, of discovery and destruction, of power and its consequences. It is a tale that continues to resonate today, as we grapple with the legacy of the atomic age and the ethical dilemmas posed by scientific progress.

In the pages that follow, we will explore the life and times of Oppenheimer, from his early years to his final days. We will delve into his scientific achievements, his political struggles, and his personal trials. We will examine his role in the development of the atomic bomb and the profound impact it had on his life and the world.

As we embark on this journey, let us remember that Oppenheimer was not just a historical figure, but a man. A man of brilliance and flaws, of courage and fear, of hope and despair. A man who, in his own words, was "torn between the scientist's pursuit of truth and the humanist's search for justice." A man who, despite his many contradictions, left an indelible mark on history. This is the enigma of Oppenheimer, a puzzle that we will attempt to piece together in the chapters to come.

TWO

The Early Years: Birth to College

On the 22nd of April in 1904, a newborn's cry joined the hum of New York City's ceaseless energy. This child, christened Julius Robert Oppenheimer, was the newest addition to an affluent, secular Jewish family. Unbeknownst to the city around him, this infant would grow to leave an indelible mark on the world far beyond the wealth and sophistication of his birthright, venturing into realms of theoretical physics and global history.

This nascent soul had the fortune of being born to Julius S. Oppenheimer and Ella Friedman Oppenheimer, each of whom would significantly mold young Robert's character and destiny. Julius, his father, was an industrious immigrant from Germany who carved a niche for himself in the world of textiles. He balanced his keen business acumen with an exquisite taste for arts and collectibles, amassing an impressive collection of minerals and paintings that he proudly displayed within their Fifth Avenue residence. This environment would serve as fertile ground, nurturing young Robert's budding interest in the aesthetics of science and art.

Ella, his mother, was not only the family's matriarch but also a passionate artist and a vibrant cultural enthusiast. A Baltimore milliner's daughter, she honed her craft at the Art Students League of New York. Her love for arts transcended the canvas, often inviting musicians and artists into their home, thereby nurturing an eclectic and culturally rich environment. This combination of her inherent creativity and dedication to the arts was instrumental in fostering Robert's appreciation for literature, philosophy, and languages.

It was in this intellectually charged environment that Oppenheimer, or "Oppie" as he was affectionately known, started showcasing signs of the extraordinary individual he would become. His early years were not confined to the traditional realms of a child's life but were expansively enriched by the family's comprehensive library, a treasure trove that quenched his ever-growing thirst for knowledge.

The family's summer escapades to their second home in Long Island further exposed Oppenheimer to a world beyond books. His engagement with the natural environment, particularly beachcombing and mineral collection, nurtured his interest in geology, which would later metamorphose into a fascination for physics.

By the time Oppenheimer was ten, he had already shown remarkable prowess in physics and chemistry. Not one to confine himself to a singular field, his intellectual curiosity also extended into the realm of literature, where he immersed himself in the world of John Donne's poetry and Charles Dickens' novels. His linguistic proficiency was also noteworthy, with him mastering French and German by the age of twelve and later adding Dutch, Italian, and Sanskrit to his remarkable linguistic repertoire.

Oppenheimer's upbringing was testament to the extraordinary prodigy he would grow into. His affluent background and the intellectual environment cultivated by his parents were the nurturing soil in which his insatiable curiosity and unparalleled intelligence blossomed.

Young Oppenheimer embarked on his academic journey at the Ethical Culture School, a learning environment that promoted self-directed exploration and curiosity. Even in these early educational experiences, the underpinnings of the intellectual tour de force that he would become were readily apparent. His passion for knowledge was a steady compass guiding him toward his next academic chapter at Harvard University.

At Harvard, he not only substantiated his intellectual brilliance but also achieved an exceptional academic feat. Within a mere span of three years, he graduated with the prestigious distinction of Summa Cum Laude. Originating from Latin, "Summa Cum Laude" translates to "with the highest honor." It is a special academic honor that educational institutions award to students who have demonstrated extraordinary academic excellence, typically by achieving the highest grades or marks among their peers.

Eager to gain more knowledge, he crossed the Atlantic and entered the Cavendish Laboratory at the University of Cambridge. Although initially finding the experimental work challenging, a move to the University of Göttingen led him into the tutelage of Max Born, a physicist of great renown. Under Born's mentorship, Oppenheimer thrived and made significant strides, with his doctoral thesis on the 'Born-Oppenheimer approximation' (a principle in quantum mechanics that simplifies the complex equations involved in molecular behavior by assuming that the motion of atomic nuclei and electrons can be separated) marking his initial foray into groundbreaking scientific contributions.

In conclusion, Oppenheimer's early life was a testament to the extraordinary achievements he would later attain. His intellectual curiosity, his affluent upbringing, and his unquenchable thirst for knowledge defined his childhood and set the stage for his future endeavors in the world of science. His remarkable intellect and passion for knowledge, honed from an early age, eventually led him to etch his name in the records of scientific history.

THREE

The Quantum Mechanic: Oppenheimer's Academic Journey

In the summer of 1922, an eager and intellectually curious 18-year-old Oppenheimer stepped onto the verdant lawns of Harvard University, marking the beginning of his extraordinary scholastic odyssey. With a head brimming with ideas and a heart bursting with a yearning to learn, he plunged into his studies. His fervor for knowledge was not limited to his chosen discipline, physics, but spilled over into chemistry, philosophy, and classics.

His peers and professors were often awestruck by Oppenheimer's scholastic pursuits. He wasn't content merely memorizing facts and figures; instead, he sought to delve into the fundamental principles that lay beneath. This knack for probing beneath the surface, seeking a deeper understanding, became a defining feature of his academic journey.

Percy Bridgman

Oppenheimer's intellectual prowess rapidly drew the attention of Harvard's distinguished faculty. Among them was Percy Bridgman, a pioneering physicist, lauded for his ground-breaking work on the effects of high pressures on materials and for his invention of an array of new experimental devices and methodologies, a feat that had earned him the Nobel Prize in Physics in 1946. Bridgman was an esteemed figure in the field, respected not only for his scientific insights but also for his commitment to teaching.

Struck by Oppenheimer's swift mastery of intricate concepts and his tendency to raise incisive questions, Bridgman perceived a unique potential in the young scholar. He saw in Oppenheimer a mind that was unafraid of complexities and that hungered for a deep and comprehensive understanding of the principles that governed the physical world. Recognizing these promising attributes, Bridgman took it upon himself to mentor the prodigious Oppenheimer.

Under Bridgman's tutelage, Oppenheimer was guided through the intricate and often bewildering maze of theoretical physics. With a mentor as accomplished as Bridgman, Oppenheimer had the unique opportunity to learn from one of the best minds in the field, an opportunity that he seized with both hands. The mentor-mentee relationship between the two was rooted in mutual respect and a shared fascination for the mysteries of the physical world.

Bridgman, known for his pedagogical innovation, employed a hands-on teaching approach that encouraged Oppenheimer to grapple directly with scientific problems. This method, aimed at gaining a comprehensive understanding of physical phenomena, resonated with Oppenheimer's own inclinations towards deep comprehension, rather than rote learning.

Beyond Academia

Outside the boundaries of classrooms and laboratories, Oppenheimer thrived in the vibrant social and intellectual scene of the Harvard Society of Fellows. This circle of young scholars engaged in passionate debates and intellectual exchanges, all of which contributed to sharpening Oppenheimer's own analytic and critical thinking skills. By the time of his graduation in 1925, he had left an indelible mark on Harvard, a testament to his exceptional academic accomplishments and intellectual prowess.

Cambridge and Göttingen

After departing the familiar halls of Harvard, Oppenheimer embarked on the next chapter of his academic voyage. The young scholar sought out the intellectual mecca of Europe, a fertile ground for his burgeoning curiosity.

In 1926, the eager 22-year-old arrived at the University of Cambridge, ready to immerse himself in the world of quantum mechanics under the guidance of J.J. Thomson, the celebrated discoverer of the electron.

Upon his arrival at the University of Cambridge, Oppenheimer found himself immersed in an atmosphere of academic rigor and prestige. However, the traditional and rigid pedagogical approach of the institution was in stark contrast to the intellectual freedom he had enjoyed at Harvard. The focus on rote learning and the adherence to established theoretical frameworks felt constraining to his fervent and inquisitive mind.

Oppenheimer yearned for an environment that could cater to his intellectual curiosities in a more holistic and personalized manner. A place where the pursuit of knowledge was not dictated by tradition but driven by curiosity and innovation. Guided by this yearning, he made the decision to move to the University of Göttingen in Germany.

Under the guiding hand of Max Born, an esteemed physicist known for his pioneering work in quantum mechanics, Oppenheimer found a learning environment that matched his desires. Göttingen, a hub of theoretical physics, was an intellectual playground teeming with pioneering minds like Werner Heisenberg, a future Nobel laureate. In this stimulating environment, surrounded by intellectual giants, Oppenheimer's own intellectual prowess was given the chance to truly flourish.

During his tenure at Göttingen, he began to make substantial strides in the realm of quantum physics. This field, in simple terms, is a branch of science that tries to explain how the tiniest particles in the universe, such as atoms and photons, behave. It suggests that at these microscopic scales, many of the rules that we take for granted in our everyday world no longer apply. Particles can exist in multiple places at the same time and even 'teleport' through barriers. This often counterintuitive science, while difficult to comprehend, underpins the workings of the universe at its most fundamental level. His publications on quantum mechanics during this period demonstrated a profound understanding of these unusual behaviors and concepts, and he was able to offer unique perspectives that differentiated him from his peers. This research was celebrated internationally, cementing Oppenheimer's standing as a major figure in the field of physics, even at such a young age.

This phase in Oppenheimer's academic journey was not just transformative but also foundational. It equipped him with a deep understanding of theoretical physics and honed his ability to challenge and expand upon established theories.

FOUR

The Berkeley Years: Teaching and Research

The Scholastic Atmosphere

As the 1920s drew to a close, the world of physics was on the brink of a monumental shift, with the University of California, Berkeley, emerging as the nucleus of this transformation. Arriving on campus in 1929, Oppenheimer, a prodigious scholar fresh from his European academic adventures, was brimming with theories and primed to apply his extensive understanding of quantum mechanics to his new role as a physics professor. His pioneering approach to education, encouraging lively discourse and dialogue, breathed fresh life into the department, sparking a dynamic environment conducive to exploration and learning.

With open arms, Berkeley embraced the arrival of Oppenheimer, the enthusiastic physicist. They awaited with bated breath the novel insights he would introduce to the field. His impressive intellect, meticulously honed under the guidance of Max Born, a luminary in quantum mechanics from the University of Göttingen, equipped him well for the vibrant scholastic ecosystem that Berkeley had to offer. Armed with a keen mind and an unquenchable passion for theoretical physics, Oppenheimer was ready to plunge into the intellectual whirlpool that Berkeley represented.

His tenure at Berkeley marked a significant chapter in Oppenheimer's intellectual narrative. During this period, he seamlessly transitioned between multiple roles: a student hungrily imbibing fresh knowledge, a professor illuminating the minds of young scholars, a researcher relentlessly pushing the frontiers of theoretical physics, and a mentor nurturing the next generation of scientists. His indelible influence permeated far beyond the physical confines of lecture halls and labs, leaving an enduring mark on the entire academic community at Berkeley. The vast range of experiences he accumulated in these formative years sculpted his persona and had a lasting impact, resonating throughout his subsequent life trajectory.

Guiding Principles: Oppenheimer's Educational Approach

The innovative nature of Oppenheimer's research was mirrored in his pedagogical philosophy and approach. He prioritized the cultivation of intellectual curiosity and the implementation of rigorous academic discipline. His teaching style echoed these principles, showcasing his immense passion and unwavering dedication to fostering intellectual development.

More than a mere provider of information, Oppenheimer acted as a mentor guiding his students on an exploratory journey into the world of physics. His classes often commenced with a provoking query or problem statement, inciting his students to engage critically with the subject matter. Oppenheimer championed a learning approach that promoted active participation and problem-solving over rote memorization.

While he held high expectations of his students, often assigning intricate problems demanding profound understanding and analytical prowess, he was equally generous with his support. He was consistently available to assist his students in deciphering the complexities of theoretical physics.

Oppenheimer's educational philosophy wasn't confined to the four walls of a classroom. He recognized learning as a continuous process and encouraged his students to cultivate their intellectual interests beyond their academic curriculum. His students were regularly invited to his home for intellectually stimulating discussions and debates, creating an atmosphere of camaraderie and intellectual unity.

In essence, Oppenheimer saw education as a journey of cultivating a lifelong love for learning and commitment to intellectual exploration. His pedagogical approach, while challenging, was highly rewarding and left an indelible mark on his students and the realm of theoretical physics.

On the Frontlines: Oppenheimer's Revolutionary Research

Oppenheimer's reputation as a giant in the field of theoretical physics grew stronger during his time at

Berkeley, as his groundbreaking research began to pave the way for his future involvement in a significant endeavor known as the Manhattan Project. This project, briefly put, was a secret U.S. government research initiative during World War II, with the goal of developing the world's first atomic bombs. The project gathered some of the brightest scientific minds of the era and ultimately led to the creation of these devastating weapons.

Oppenheimer focused his research efforts at Berkeley on quantum mechanics, a field that was in its nascent stages during the 1920s and 1930s. His fascination with cosmic rays—high-energy particles from space that interact with Earth's atmosphere—yielded groundbreaking research, offering new perspectives on these intriguing particles.

In addition to his work on cosmic rays, Oppenheimer significantly impacted nuclear physics. He was among the pioneering scientists to hypothesize the existence of black holes, an idea initially greeted with skepticism but later recognized as a fundamental concept in astrophysics. His exploratory research on neutron stars and white dwarfs greatly enriched our understanding of these celestial entities and their cosmic roles.

Oppenheimer's research was marked by a blend of inventive thinking and rigorous scientific methods. His penchant for challenging conventional theories and stretching the boundaries of scientific understanding made his work at times contentious, but always innovative and intellectually stimulating.

Despite the intricate nature of his research, Oppenheimer possessed an extraordinary ability to convey complex scientific principles in a comprehensible manner. His lectures were renowned for their lucidity and precision, and his writings mirrored this clarity and captivation.

He excelled at demystifying abstract concepts, making the enigmas of the universe understandable to the layperson.

Personal Struggles and Triumphs: Oppenheimer's Life Beyond the Laboratory

The complexity of his personal life matched the variety in his professional engagements, etched with an array of ups and downs that sculpted his identity.

A man of immense talent, Oppenheimer had varied interests spanning from a deep love for poetry and philosophy to an affinity for the arts and music. He often utilized his leisure time exploring art exhibitions or indulging in concerts. His thirst for knowledge was not limited to physics but spanned a variety of fields, marking him as a multifaceted intellectual. Quoting Bhagavad Gita and conversing in French and German, he mirrored a global and philosophical perspective in his thoughts. These diverse interests infused a creative edge into his scientific pursuits, enabling him to interlink distinct disciplines. Amidst his vast intellectual capabilities and accomplishments, Oppenheimer faced his share of personal dilemmas and insecurities, which lent an intricate facet to his character. However, these layers did not eclipse his brilliance but added a profound depth to his persona.

The road that Oppenheimer walked was not devoid of obstacles. He was a complex individual, possessing a brilliant mind that was at times overshadowed by emotional turmoil. His bouts of depression were well known to those close to him. This mental health struggle presented a formidable challenge in his life, often leaving him feeling despondent and disconnected. Yet, Oppenheimer showed a remarkable ability to persevere and channel his energies into his work, even during the darkest periods of his life.

Alongside his depression, Oppenheimer had a reputation for a fiery temper. His quick intellect and cutting wit could turn sharp and argumentative, which frequently put him at odds with colleagues and friends. This aspect of his personality led to a number of contentious interactions and professional disagreements. Despite these episodes, his brilliance was often enough to mend strained relationships and maintain his standing in the scientific community.

Central among these relationships was his matrimony with Katherine "Kitty" Puening, a fascinating character in her own right. She was a biologist by training, a staunch leftist, and a divorced mother of a young son when she crossed paths with Oppenheimer at the University of California, Berkeley, where they both worked. Their union was laced with tension due to their contrasting political ideologies, but they also shared a love for science and intellectual pursuits.

His turbulent marriage to Kitty, despite its disharmony, blessed him with two beloved children. Their firstborn, Peter, embraced a life deeply connected to nature, becoming a furniture maker and cattle rancher. Their younger child, Katherine, known as "Toni," was a passionate student of history who inherited her parents' intellectual curiosity. Tragically, Toni's life was cut short in 1977, when she died from an apparent suicide, a devastating blow that cast a long shadow over the family's later years. He nurtured close bonds with many who admired his intellectual brilliance and enthusiasm for learning.

Oppenheimer's life outside the lab strikingly paralleled his professional trajectory. Much like his navigation through the labyrinth of theoretical physics, he tackled the complexities of his personal life with the same resilience.

In conclusion, Oppenheimer's years at Berkeley set the stage for his future achievements and challenges. They were a formative period that left an indelible mark on his life and career. They were the years that shaped Julius Robert Oppenheimer, the man and the physicist, and they will forever be remembered as a defining chapter in the history of theoretical physics.

FIVE

The Political Awakening: Oppenheimer's Ideological Shift

Oppenheimer's life unfurled against the backdrop of the 20th-century world, a period steeped in geopolitical convulsions, devastating wars, and seismic ideological shifts. It was within this tempest that Oppenheimer's political philosophy emerged and evolved, shifting him from an apolitical scientist to a politically-engaged figure.

. . .

Embarking on a Journey: Oppenheimer's Early Life

Born into a wealthy, secular Jewish family in 1904, Oppenheimer's early life was sheltered from the economic hardships that often act as catalysts for political awareness. Instead, he enjoyed an environment that fostered intellectual curiosity and the freedom to explore the mysteries of the physical world. His family's liberal leanings - advocating for education, social justice, and intellectual pursuits - were subtly imprinted on young Oppenheimer, laying the foundation for his later ideological transformation.

However, during his formative years and early tenure at Harvard University, Oppenheimer displayed little interest in politics. Instead, he was captivated by the field of quantum mechanics, preferring to delve into subatomic particles' mysteries rather than the intricacies of governmental machinations. His political consciousness was dormant during these years, awaiting the right conditions to stir and awaken.

One key aspect of Oppenheimer's early life that would later influence his political transformation was his interest in Eastern philosophy.

His deep fascination with the Bhagavad Gita, which he read and understood in its original Sanskrit, helped broaden his worldview, providing a philosophical underpinning that would subtly influence his political maturation.

Catalysts for Change: The Awakening of Political Consciousness

Oppenheimer's political maturation was not an isolated process but rather a response to the tumultuous socio-political events that marked the 1930s and 1940s.

The first major catalyst was the economic devastation wrought by the Great Depression. Witnessing the dire poverty and widespread unemployment, Oppenheimer was jolted from his privileged existence and began to question the capitalist system that had enabled such calamity.

The second impetus came from across the Atlantic. Fascism's rise in Europe, particularly the horrors perpetrated by Nazi Germany against Jews, resonated personally with Oppenheimer, despite his secular upbringing. These atrocities underscored the necessity of political engagement and the imperative for robust and fair governance.

The final catalyst for change came closer to home. Upon his move to the University of California, Berkeley, in the 1930s, Oppenheimer came in contact with the Communist Party. He encountered a passionate group of intellectuals and activists advocating social justice and equality - a stark contrast to the inequalities laid bare by the Great Depression. Their fervor inspired him, stirring his political consciousness and prompting his alignment with their cause.

From Detached Observer to Political Advocate: The Metamorphosis

As Oppenheimer's political views took form, he transitioned from a detached observer to a politically engaged scientist. His time at Berkeley proved crucial to this transformation, with its vibrant political atmosphere nurturing his evolving convictions. While there's no conclusive evidence of his official membership in the Communist Party, his attendance at meetings, financial contributions, and hosting of party gatherings at his home suggest a deep alignment with their ideologies.

Oppenheimer's political engagement was not confined to the boundaries of party politics. He became involved in broader societal issues, protesting against the rise of fascism in Europe and collaborating with union organizers. These activities reflected his belief in collective action and the potential for societal change, demonstrating his willingness to use his influential status to amplify these causes.

Significantly, Oppenheimer's political maturation began to influence his professional life. He recognized the societal implications of his scientific research, particularly in the field of nuclear physics.

This realization influenced his decision to lead the Manhattan Project - an endeavor he viewed as a means to counter the potential threat of Nazi Germany's rumored atomic bomb project.

As the leader of the Manhattan Project, he had two main roles: a scientific one and an administrative one. In his scientific role, he coordinated the research efforts of numerous scientists in fields such as physics, chemistry, and engineering. He oversaw the progress of their work, directed the scientific goals, and handled any problems that came up. In his administrative role, Oppenheimer managed the project's resources and personnel. This included running the main research facility at Los Alamos, New Mexico, and collaborating with other research and production centers across the U.S. He was also responsible for reporting progress and challenges to military and political leaders, ensuring they understood the technical aspects of the project.

His acceptance of this role represented a tangible manifestation of his political beliefs and marked a significant departure from his previous apolitical stance.

Post-War Politics and Legacy: A Life Interwoven with Politics

In the aftermath of World War II, Oppenheimer found himself in the epicenter of political debates around nuclear power. A vocal advocate for the international control of nuclear power, he vehemently opposed the development of the hydrogen bomb. This stance underscored the intertwined nature of his scientific work and political beliefs, which had evolved significantly from his earlier years of political indifference.

However, his political journey was not without tribulation. The height of this challenge came in 1954, during the infamous security hearing where Oppenheimer's loyalty to the United States was questioned due to his previous affiliations with the Communist Party. This ordeal had a profound impact on his career and further complicated his relationship with politics.

In sum, Oppenheimer's narrative paints a rich, multifaceted picture of an individual at the confluence of science and politics. His journey, shaped by the ideological currents of his time, offers profound insights into the interplay between personal convictions and world events, reminding us of the influential power of ideas in shaping our world.

Unfolding Legacy: The Indelible Imprint of Oppenheimer's Political Transformation

The journey of Oppenheimer's ideological metamorphosis has left an indelible imprint, extending far beyond his personal life and seeping into the grand narrative of global history. The creation of the atomic bomb, a direct result of the Manhattan Project he helmed, altered the face of warfare and dictated the course of international politics. The sheer magnitude of its destructive capabilities became an ominous focal point during the Cold War, and the moral discourse surrounding its deployment continues to engage thinkers today.

On the domestic front, however, Oppenheimer's political past would resurface, casting a long shadow over his career. During the fever pitch of the Red Scare, his prior associations with the Communist Party turned into a weapon against him. In the crucible of a security hearing, he was stripped of his clearance, effectively muting his voice in the spheres of policy-making.

Yet, even when faced with this personal setback, Oppenheimer remained steadfast in his convictions. He continued to champion the peaceful application of nuclear technology and stressed the importance of controlling nuclear weapons proliferation.

His metamorphosis from an academic physicist to a politically engaged scientist had come full circle, leaving a resonating legacy within the intertwined realms of science and politics.

Oppenheimer's transformative journey from the realms of the apolitical into the heart of political engagement serves as a compelling testament to the intricate dance between personal beliefs and global affairs. It showcases the power of individual determination amidst sweeping historical events, offering a vivid portrayal of how political awakenings can leave a mark on not just the lives of individuals, but also the trajectory of the world. As we conclude this chapter, we acknowledge the lasting impact and transformative power of this personal political journey, a series of actions and decisions that irrefutably secured Oppenheimer's place in the chronicles of human civilization.

SIX

The Manhattan Project: The Birth of the Atomic Bomb

Origins of the Manhattan Project

As the dawn of the 1940s descended upon a world besieged by the calamity of the Second World War, the menace of Adolf Hitler's Nazi Germany dominated global fears. Reports of the Nazis' intensive research into nuclear fission fueled an escalating dread that they were on the precipice of developing a weapon of mass destruction—an atomic bomb. It was against this backdrop that the seeds of the Manhattan Project were sown, setting in motion a series of events that would irrevocably alter the course of human history.

The inception of the Manhattan Project can be traced back to a momentous letter, penned by the renowned physicist Albert Einstein in August 1939. Einstein, despite his pacifist leanings, was alarmed by the potential implications of the groundbreaking discovery of nuclear fission by German chemists Otto Hahn and Fritz Strassmann in 1938. He feared that this discovery might equip Hitler's regime with the scientific knowledge necessary to construct an atomic weapon, a prospect that would dramatically shift the balance of power in the war.

Moved by these concerns, Einstein composed a letter to the then-President of the United States, Franklin D. Roosevelt. This pivotal correspondence, often referred to as the "Einstein-Szilárd letter," was also signed by Hungarian physicist Leó Szilárd, who shared Einstein's concerns.

The letter detailed the potential of a new type of bomb, one that harnessed the energy released by nuclear fission, resulting in an explosion far surpassing the destructive power of any weapon hitherto known. More importantly, it urged the United States to expedite its own research into nuclear energy to safeguard against the looming German threat.

The Einstein-Szilárd letter, along with the intensifying global conflict, served as the catalyst for the Manhattan Project. By late 1941, under the guidance of the Roosevelt administration, the United States embarked on the most ambitious and secretive scientific endeavor of the time—the race to develop an atomic bomb. The project would draw on the collective intellectual prowess of some of the greatest minds of the era, culminating in a weapon of unparalleled power.

An Unlikely Leader

The Manhattan Project was a mammoth undertaking, demanding not just a profound scientific mind, but a leader who could navigate the labyrinth of complex human dynamics and bureaucratic challenges inherent in such a colossal endeavor. As the search for a suitable scientific director commenced, one name began to stand out from the rest: J. Robert Oppenheimer. Despite his relative youth and lack of administrative experience, Oppenheimer was an unconventional choice that would prove to be pivotal in the project's success.

At the onset, Oppenheimer's appointment was met with skepticism. His academic career, albeit impressive, was mainly confined to the realm of theoretical physics, with no significant leadership roles or large-scale project management experience under his belt. Moreover, he was still in his late thirties, considerably younger than many of the seasoned scientists who would be working under him.

However, what Oppenheimer lacked in administrative experience, he compensated for with a combination of personal attributes that made him uniquely qualified for this unprecedented leadership role. Firstly, his charisma and eloquence were unparalleled. Colleagues and students alike were often entranced by his captivating lectures, his ability to distill complex concepts into comprehensible language, and his unyielding passion for the mysteries of the universe. This charisma would prove invaluable in fostering unity among a diverse group of scientists and maintaining morale amid the project's relentless pressures.

Secondly, Oppenheimer was known for his broad interdisciplinary knowledge. His intellectual curiosity was not confined to the domain of theoretical physics but sprawled across a spectrum of disciplines from philosophy to Eastern literature. This intellectual breadth enabled him to approach problems from multiple perspectives, fostering a creative, collaborative environment that was instrumental in overcoming the scientific and technical hurdles that the Manhattan Project posed.

Moreover, Oppenheimer had a remarkable ability to inspire those around him. His relentless dedication to his work, his ability to think outside the box, and his unwavering commitment to the project's success were infectious. His leadership style fostered a sense of camaraderie and shared purpose among the project members, transforming a collection of brilliant individuals into a cohesive, productive team.

Lastly, Oppenheimer's appointment was strongly advocated by General Leslie Groves, the military head of the project.

Groves recognized in Oppenheimer a kindred spirit of sorts - someone with a vision and the determination to see it through. Despite reservations from others due to Oppenheimer's previous left-leaning political affiliations, Groves pushed for his appointment. This alliance between the military and science, embodied in the relationship between Groves and Oppenheimer, would prove crucial in the progression of the Manhattan Project.Thus, in 1942, Oppenheimer was appointed as the scientific director of the Manhattan Project. This marked the commencement of an intense chapter in his life, one that would see him navigate uncharted territories, and grapple with unprecedented ethical dilemmas.

Hurdling Obstacles: The Scientific and Logistical Challenges of the Manhattan Project

The path to the atomic bomb was far from straightforward. In its course, the Manhattan Project would grapple with enormous scientific and logistical challenges.

From theoretical hurdles to practical setbacks, each phase of the project was laden with difficulties that demanded ingenious solutions and herculean efforts from its team.

Among the scientific challenges was the very crux of the project: the controlled release of atomic energy. The project's task required not just theoretical understanding, but also practical implementation of nuclear fission on a scale never before attempted. The enormity of this scientific undertaking was exacerbated by the paucity of previous research in the field and the unavailability of a proven blueprint to guide the project's direction.

Key breakthroughs often emerged from grappling with these obstacles. For example, the team had to devise a method for producing and purifying the necessary fissionable materials, primarily plutonium and uranium-235. Solving this issue was a gargantuan task, requiring an amalgamation of chemistry, physics, and engineering. However, they succeeded in designing and constructing full-scale nuclear reactors and separation facilities, marking a significant scientific and technological achievement.

Logistical challenges were equally daunting. The project necessitated the construction of vast facilities spread across the United States, including those at Oak Ridge, Tennessee, and Hanford, Washington. The task of coordinating the operations of these disparate locations, all while maintaining utmost secrecy, was Herculean. Managing the project's sprawling resources and workforce, which at its peak numbered 130,000, further added to the complexity.

Moreover, the project existed within the crucible of war and the weight of its mission cast a heavy burden on all involved. The scientists were not immune to the ethical and moral implications of their work, leading to a distinct undercurrent of tension that permeated the project's lifespan.

At the helm of these challenges stood Oppenheimer. His leadership and ability to synthesize knowledge from a broad spectrum of scientific disciplines proved instrumental in guiding the project to its completion.

Oppenheimer's interdisciplinary intellect was vital in fostering an environment of collaboration, ensuring that chemists, physicists, engineers, and mathematicians effectively cooperated to overcome the challenges that arose. He effectively used his charisma to maintain morale and promote unity among the project's diverse personnel, making certain that each challenge was met with a concerted effort.

A testament to Oppenheimer's leadership was his handling of the project's most significant technical challenge: designing a practical bomb. The team under his leadership proposed two different designs - the "Little Boy", a relatively straightforward gun-type fission bomb using uranium-235, and the more complex "Fat Man", an implosion-type fission bomb using plutonium. The latter design necessitated extraordinary creativity and cooperation from the scientists, given its novel and untested nature.

The journey was arduous, fraught with scientific uncertainties, logistical nightmares, and ethical dilemmas. Yet, the Manhattan Project, under the leadership of the unlikely figure of Oppenheimer, navigated these hurdles, forever altering the course of history in the process.

Life Under Secrecy: The Establishment and Culture of Los Alamos Laboratory

In the desolate mesas of New Mexico, a secret city sprung up seemingly overnight, built to house the minds that would pioneer the atomic age. Los Alamos, a secluded location chosen for its remote geographical positioning, became the crucible for the Manhattan Project and the setting for some of the most significant scientific undertakings of the 20th century.

The establishment of Los Alamos Laboratory, or Project Y, as it was referred to then, was carried out under a veil of utmost secrecy. The remote boys' school on the site was quickly transformed into a sprawling research facility, complete with living quarters for the scientists and their families. This rapid development was fueled by the urgency of the war and the high-stakes nature of their mission.

Living and working conditions in Los Alamos were Spartan, especially in the initial days. Accommodations were rudimentary, with many families living in hastily built wooden houses or even converted barracks. Basic amenities were scarce and residents had to contend with the harsh New Mexico environment. Moreover, the isolation, both physical and intellectual, was a significant challenge. Contact with the outside world was restricted, and even within the facility, the principle of compartmentalization meant that many scientists only knew about the specific part of the project they were working on.

Yet, despite these hardships, Los Alamos developed a unique culture. The forced intimacy of the secluded environment fostered a close-knit community, leading to a remarkable camaraderie among the scientists and their families. The intellectual atmosphere was electric, with some of the brightest minds of the time collaborating and clashing in their pursuit of a common goal.

Security measures at Los Alamos were unparalleled. The site was heavily guarded and all correspondence, even with family members outside, was censored. Visitors were rare and carefully vetted. Every resident had an alias, and to the outside world, the entire laboratory was only known as a nondescript P.O. Box – "Box 1663, Santa Fe, New Mexico." The weight of their work, coupled with the stringent security, created a palpable tension that permeated life at Los Alamos.

Despite these hardships and constraints, the residents of Los Alamos persevered. They organized social events like dances and parties and even published a community newspaper named "The Los Alamos Primer." Such endeavors humanized life at the secret laboratory, fostering a sense of normalcy amidst the extraordinary.

Los Alamos was a study in contrasts – a clandestine facility tucked away in an obscure corner of the world, yet standing at the frontier of human knowledge. Here, Oppenheimer and his team undertook a task of monumental proportions, their work and lives cloaked in secrecy. This extraordinary chapter in Oppenheimer's life, framed by the unique backdrop of Los Alamos, formed the linchpin of his journey during the Manhattan Project.

SEVEN

The Trinity Test and the Culmination of the Manhattan Project

The long and arduous path of the Manhattan Project converged into a singular, transformative moment at precisely 5:29:45 a.m. on July 16, 1945. This was the instant the world's first atomic bomb, understatedly known as the "Gadget," was successfully detonated in a test code-named "Trinity." The detonation was the outcome of years of exhaustive effort, unwavering perseverance, and unprecedented collaboration. The reverberations of this event echoed throughout history, forever altering the dynamics of warfare and showcasing humanity's unprecedented capability for both creation and destruction.

The test site for this historical event was the secluded Alamogordo Bombing Range nestled within the desolate expanse of New Mexico's Jornada del Muerto desert. There, the Gadget was hoisted aloft on a 100-foot-tall steel tower, a hub of scientific instruments and monitoring equipment sprawled out below, their vigilant electronic eyes primed to record this potentially world-changing event.

As the first hints of dawn seeped into the sky, a collective of scientists and military personnel hunkered down in concrete and steel shelters scattered across the range. The countdown began, and with every passing second, an air of intense anticipation and gravitas filled the New Mexico desert. This was the moment of truth for the Manhattan Project.

Suddenly, at the designated hour, a brilliant, blinding flash punctured the semi-darkness, instantly replaced by an engulfing fireball. The surrounding desert was bathed in an ethereal light, hotter than the surface of the sun. A colossal mushroom cloud, the grim signature of atomic energy, soon rose high above the detonation site, soaring to 38,000 feet within minutes. The unleashed power equated to 20 kilotons of TNT, far outstripping the initial estimates of most project participants.

Standing at a remove, Oppenheimer watched this awe-inspiring spectacle unfold. The sheer might and dread of the detonation prompted a visceral reaction, where relief and pride were laced with an unnerving apprehension. The sight stirred in Oppenheimer's mind a haunting line from the Bhagavad Gita, a verse from ancient Hindu scripture: "Now I am become Death, the destroyer of worlds."

This somber thought seemed a fitting reflection on the terrifying destructive force they had just unleashed.

Oppenheimer's response encapsulates the stark paradox that was the Trinity test. On the one hand, it was a testament to human ingenuity, a triumphant milestone in scientific achievement. On the other, it revealed a harrowing new potential for destruction, an unsettling demonstration to mankind's ability to engineer its own annihilation.

The resounding success of the Trinity test signaled the completion of the Manhattan Project. Yet, it also marked the onset of an era laden with complex moral, political, and societal dilemmas. With the atomic age dawning, scientists like Oppenheimer were thrust into the limelight, lauded for their achievements but also beset with the burden of the future. As the world reveled in the breakthrough, these architects of the nuclear age were already grappling with the profound implications of their creation. This convergence of accomplishment and concern encapsulated the concluding moments of the Manhattan Project, setting the stage for humanity's next great challenge - life in the nuclear era.

The Atomic Bomb's Unprecedented Impact: Hiroshima, Nagasaki, and the End of World War II

Only weeks after the triumphant yet chilling Trinity test, the power of the atomic bomb was unleashed upon the world in an act of unparalleled devastation. The American B-29 bomber, aptly named Enola Gay, took off from Tinian Island in the Pacific Ocean on August 6, 1945. Its mission was to drop the first atomic bomb used in warfare, named "Little Boy," over the Japanese city of Hiroshima.

At 8:15 a.m. local time, the people of Hiroshima experienced a calamity unlike any the world had seen. The city was swallowed by an intense flash of light, followed by an unprecedented explosion. In an instant, the heart of Hiroshima was decimated, over two-thirds of its buildings obliterated, and tens of thousands of its inhabitants killed. The survivors, often gravely injured, found themselves in a desolate wasteland, their city replaced by a scarred and radioactive ruin.

A mere three days later, a second atomic bomb, this one named "Fat Man," was dropped on the city of Nagasaki, wreaking similar destruction. By the end of 1945, the combined death toll from the immediate blast, injuries, and radiation sickness was estimated to be over 200,000, a figure that would continue to rise due to long-term radiation effects.

The dropping of these atomic bombs precipitated Japan's unconditional surrender, marking the end of World War II. From the perspective of the Allied forces, the bombs had served their purpose, bringing a swift end to a brutal conflict that had claimed millions of lives.

However, the cataclysmic destruction wrought by these bombs ignited profound moral and ethical dilemmas.

The sheer scale of destruction and the indiscriminate nature of the casualties stirred a profound debate that continues to this day. While the bombs indisputably helped end the war, they also ushered in an age where human civilization had acquired the means for its own annihilation. The haunting imagery of Hiroshima and Nagasaki stands as a grim reminder of this newfound power, a warning from history about the potential consequences of scientific advancement when wedded to warfare.

In the aftermath, Oppenheimer, the "father of the atomic bomb," was faced with a profound moral quandary.

While the successful development of the atomic bomb represented a remarkable scientific achievement, its devastating impact on Hiroshima and Nagasaki weighed heavily on him. He had led the development of a weapon that, while instrumental in ending the most widespread war in human history, had inflicted unimaginable suffering and marked the advent of an era where the prospect of global annihilation was a constant threat.

The bomb had a transformative impact on Oppenheimer, deeply affecting his perspective on his role as a scientist. The events further galvanized his commitment to a peaceful, controlled use of atomic energy and arms regulation. He came to advocate for international control of nuclear weapons and became a voice of conscience, reminding the world of the moral responsibilities that came with such destructive power.

The end of World War II, thus, marked a new beginning—an age defined by nuclear capabilities, shadowed by the devastation of Hiroshima and Nagasaki, and steered by the moral, ethical, and political decisions that would shape the world's approach to this unprecedented power. In this new era, figures like Oppenheimer would continue to play a vital role, not just as scientists, but also as guardians of human conscience and responsibility.

EIGHT

Reflections: The Ambivalence of the Atomic Architect

In the aftermath of the detonations over Hiroshima and Nagasaki, Oppenheimer found himself in a paradoxical position - hailed as a hero for his scientific leadership in bringing World War II to a swift conclusion, while also bearing the weight of responsibility for a weapon that ushered in a new era of potential global annihilation.

Oppenheimer's feelings about the Manhattan Project and the atomic bombs it produced were complex and evolved over time. Immediately after the successful Trinity test, he was reported to have reacted with a mix of satisfaction and foreboding. His brother, Frank, remembered him saying simply, "It worked." However, Oppenheimer himself later recalled that a verse from the Hindu scripture Bhagavad Gita came to mind: "Now I am become Death, the destroyer of worlds." This poignant reflection revealed his acute awareness of the magnitude of what he and his team had accomplished and the potential consequences it held for the world.

The bombings of Hiroshima and Nagasaki deeply affected Oppenheimer. The scale of devastation and the human toll brought home the stark reality of atomic warfare. In October 1945, he visited President Harry S. Truman in the White House, where he expressed his regret, reportedly saying, "Mr. President, I feel I have blood on my hands."

This statement revealed a man grappling with guilt and the moral implications of his work. Truman, taken aback by this display of remorse, reportedly told his secretary of state later that he never wanted to see that "cry-baby scientist" in his office again.

Throughout the subsequent years, Oppenheimer's reflections on his role in the development of the atomic bomb were marked by a blend of pride, guilt, and a deep sense of responsibility. He was proud of the scientific achievement the Manhattan Project represented and the role it played in ending the war. However, he was also conscious that this same work had led to an unprecedented loss of life and had given humanity the means for its own destruction.

Oppenheimer became an advocate for international control of nuclear weapons and a staunch opponent of the development of the hydrogen bomb. He was the voice that urged for the use of science for peaceful means, testifying before Congress, giving public speeches, and working with international committees. His transformation from a theoretical physicist to the scientific director of the Manhattan Project and finally to a statesman advocating for nuclear regulation underscored his evolving views on his role and responsibilities as a scientist in the atomic age.

In a 1965 television interview, Oppenheimer reflected,

> *"I have no remorse about the making of the bomb and Trinity... That was done right. As for how we used it, I understand why it happened and appreciate with what nobility those men with whom I'd worked made their decision. But I do not have the feeling that it was done right. The ultimatum to Japan [the Potsdam Declaration demanding Japan's surrender] was full of pious platitudes... our government should have acted with more foresight and clarity..."*

In summary, Oppenheimer's reflections on his role in the Manhattan Project and the use of the atomic bomb were a complex interplay of pride in scientific achievement, regret over the enormous loss of life, and an increasingly nuanced understanding of the ethical responsibilities of scientists. His journey illuminates the moral dilemmas faced by scientists working at the cutting edge of technology and warfare, a theme that is as relevant today as it was in the dawn of the nuclear age.

. . .

Legacy of the Manhattan Project: Unraveling the Threads of the Nuclear Age

The Manhattan Project, with its successful development and use of atomic weapons, decisively ended World War II and simultaneously opened a new, daunting chapter in human history - the Nuclear Age.

This period has been characterized by a fundamental reimagining of warfare, political power dynamics, scientific responsibility, and humanity's relationship with technology. The Manhattan Project's enduring legacy can be traced along these multiple dimensions, each carrying the indelible imprint of Oppenheimer and his team's extraordinary endeavor.

The conclusion of World War II brought little reprieve from global tensions, as a new geopolitical landscape rapidly emerged, defined by ideological divisions between the United States and the Soviet Union. The atomic bombs dropped on Hiroshima and Nagasaki were not just a destructive show of force but a harbinger of the potential power struggles in this emerging bipolar world order. The possession of nuclear weapons became synonymous with global dominance and strategic advantage, leading to an unprecedented arms race between the superpowers during the Cold War.

The United States and the Soviet Union plunged into a relentless pursuit of developing more potent and efficient nuclear weapons, resulting in a terrifying buildup of arsenals on both sides. The threat of Mutual Assured Destruction (MAD), where a full-scale use of nuclear weapons by two or more opposing sides would cause the complete annihilation of both the attacker and the defender, became a chilling deterrent that paradoxically maintained a precarious peace.

This nuclear arms race wasn't limited to military applications. Civilian nuclear energy programs emerged, heralding the promise of unlimited power. The atom, which had shown its destructive potential in the bleakest terms, was also touted as a beacon of progress and prosperity. Nuclear energy was seen as the solution to the world's growing power needs, leading to the establishment of nuclear power plants worldwide.

But the devastating accidents at Three Mile Island, Chernobyl, and Fukushima underscored the inherent risks associated with nuclear energy.

Three Mile Island: On March 28, 1979, the Three Mile Island nuclear facility in Pennsylvania, United States, experienced a partial meltdown in its second reactor. A combination of equipment malfunctions, design-related problems, and operator errors led to the release of radioactive gases into the environment, though the overall impact was limited by the containment structure. Despite no immediate deaths or injuries, the incident brought about widespread fear and mistrust, leading to significant changes in nuclear regulatory policies in the U.S.

Chernobyl: The Chernobyl disaster took place on April 26, 1986, at the No. 4 reactor in the Chernobyl Nuclear Power Plant, near the city of Pripyat in the north of the Ukrainian SSR in the Soviet Union. A safety test simulating a power outage, which included shutting down the emergency safety systems, led to an uncontrolled nuclear chain reaction. This resulted in a catastrophic nuclear explosion and subsequent fires that released a significant amount of radioactive particles into the atmosphere. The event directly caused around 31 deaths, while long-term effects, including cancer and deformities, are estimated to have caused thousands of deaths.

Fukushima: Triggered by a massive 9.0-magnitude earthquake and ensuing tsunami on March 11, 2011, the Fukushima Daiichi nuclear disaster was the most significant nuclear incident since Chernobyl. The natural disaster cut off power to the plant and disabled the cooling systems for three nuclear reactors, leading to meltdowns and the release of radioactive materials. The incident caused no immediate deaths due to radiation exposure, but the evacuation and displacement of people affected by the disaster have been linked to over a thousand deaths. The long-term effects on human health and the environment are still being studied.

These incidents ignited heated debates about the viability and safety of nuclear power, discussions that continue to shape energy policies today. At the heart of these debates lies the Manhattan Project's dual legacy - the allure of harnessing the atom's immense power and the ever-present risk of cataclysmic disaster.

In the realm of science, the Manhattan Project radically transformed the perception of scientific research and its societal implications. It demonstrated how scientific advancements, driven by state resources and guided by military objectives, could shape global events. The ethical dilemmas faced by the scientists involved in the Manhattan Project continue to resonate with contemporary scientists, particularly those involved in developing advanced technologies with potential dual-use dilemmas, such as artificial intelligence and genetic engineering.

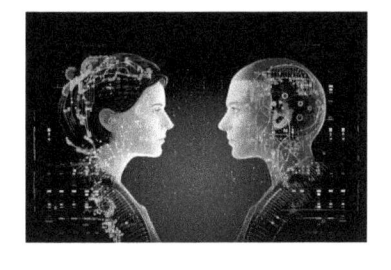

The Manhattan Project, under Oppenheimer's stewardship, is a testament to human ingenuity and a stark reminder of our capacity for destruction. It sparked the dawn of the Nuclear Age, a period that has profoundly influenced international relations, scientific research, and the way we perceive our place in the universe. The project's legacy is a deeply woven part of our shared global history, its threads continuing to unfold and shape our present and future. As we continue to grapple with these issues, the lessons learned from the Manhattan Project and Oppenheimer's reflections serve as valuable guideposts in navigating the complex interface of science, ethics, and society.

NINE

Later Life and Career

Following the completion of the Manhattan Project and the tumultuous end of the Second World War, Oppenheimer's career trajectory took a new direction. From the secretive military laboratories to the hallowed halls of academia, Oppenheimer ventured into an entirely different realm. In this chapter, we delve into Oppenheimer's life post-Manhattan Project, exploring his professorial career, his leadership at the Institute for

Advanced Study (IAS) in Princeton, and his enduring contributions to theoretical physics.

From War to Peace: Oppenheimer's Return to Academia

With the end of the war, Oppenheimer found himself at a crossroads. He had spearheaded a project that had forever altered the face of warfare and had ramifications that shook the very core of human ethics and morality. Although he was initially appointed to a high-ranking position on the United States Atomic Energy Commission (AEC), his heart lay in academia, and he decided to return to it.

As a professor at the University of California, Berkeley, Oppenheimer resumed teaching and research, his charisma and intellect continuing to leave a lasting impression on his students. However, the war had undeniably transformed him. No longer merely an academic, he strived to instill in his students an understanding of the societal implications of their work, drawing from his personal experiences during the Manhattan Project.

Leading the Intellectual Vanguard: Institute for Advanced Study

In 1947, Oppenheimer was appointed the Director of the Institute for Advanced Study in Princeton, a post he held until 1966.

The IAS was an intellectual hub, home to some of the greatest minds of the 20th century, including Albert Einstein. As director, Oppenheimer aimed to foster an environment that encouraged the free pursuit of knowledge and interdisciplinary collaboration.

Under his stewardship, the IAS grew in stature, attracting world-renowned scholars from diverse fields. Oppenheimer's vision played a significant role in shaping the IAS into a leading center for theoretical research. Although he faced some criticism regarding his administrative style and decision-making, his passion for knowledge and his conviction that pure research could offer profound insights remained unwavering.

Oppenheimer and Theoretical Physics

Despite the administrative duties at IAS and the political turmoil he later faced during the Red Scare, Oppenheimer remained a physicist at heart. He continued to make meaningful contributions to theoretical physics, specifically in quantum field theory and astrophysics.

Among his most notable post-war scientific contributions was his work, alongside his student

Hartland Snyder, on gravitational collapse. Their research paved the way for the theoretical prediction of black holes, astronomical objects that have since been empirically observed and have become central to our understanding of the universe.

TEN

The Red Scare and Oppenheimer's Fall from Grace

The 1950s were a period marked by paranoia and fear, where the Cold War was reaching its zenith and an obsessive dread of communism consumed the United States. It was in this turbulent era that Oppenheimer, once revered as a pioneering scientist and national hero, found himself ensnared in a web of suspicion and doubt.

. . .

The Erosion of a National Icon

Oppenheimer, the acclaimed architect of the atomic bomb, witnessed his public image slowly but surely disintegrate. Whispers of his alleged Communist Party membership during the 1930s began to circulate, tarnishing his reputation. The man who was once universally lauded was now subjected to an inquisition of his past affiliations and ideologies, which in turn posed questions about his loyalty and intellectual freedom.

Accusations of Treachery

In the frosty climate of the escalating Cold War, accusations of espionage and communist sympathies were leveled against Oppenheimer. These allegations, though severe, were primarily based on his past connections with identified communists and his vocal disapproval of the hydrogen bomb's development.

Among the multitude of charges, one particularly damaging accusation came from a former student, William Perl. He claimed that Oppenheimer had encouraged him to leak classified information to the

Soviets. Despite the absence of concrete proof, this assertion did considerable harm to Oppenheimer's standing. Oppenheimer's predicament was further compounded when he confessed to lying about his contacts with communists to security officials, intensifying the existing mistrust.

The Theater of Judgement: Oppenheimer's Hearing

Spring 1954 saw the commencement of Oppenheimer's security hearing in Washington D.C. This courtroom drama unfolded before a captive audience composed of spectators, journalists, and government officials, all of whom were eager to witness the potential downfall of a scientific luminary.

Throughout the trial, Oppenheimer managed to retain his equanimity. His defense was spearheaded by the astute attorney Lloyd Garrison, who painted a picture of Oppenheimer as a patriot victimized by political machinations and irrational paranoia. Despite the determined efforts of his defense, the prosecution painted him as a treacherous figure guilty of espionage and a threat to national security.

A Stinging Verdict and Its Repercussions

On June 29, 1954, the decisive verdict was announced: Oppenheimer's security clearance was withdrawn. The reverberations of this decision echoed across the nation and the globe, permanently staining his professional career and personal reputation.

The charges that had precipitated this outcome—espionage, communist associations, betrayal—were severe. Even though the evidence supporting them was circumstantial at best, the pervading climate of fear during the Cold War era amplified their significance.

In the aftermath of the trial, Oppenheimer, once a titan in the realm of American science, found himself confronting widespread condemnation, even from those who had once been his close associates. Nevertheless, despite this severe blow, Oppenheimer remained a colossal figure in the scientific community. His narrative is one of persistence and relentless pursuit of knowledge, even in the face of significant adversity.

Reflection on the Legacy of the Hearing

The 1954 security hearing remains a somber episode in Oppenheimer's life.

It stands as a demonstration of a society caught in a tumultuous whirlwind of paranoia and political maneuvering. Despite the immense personal and professional costs, Oppenheimer's narrative remains one of resilience. His legacy stands undiminished, a beacon of scientific curiosity and achievement amidst political upheaval. His fall from grace was harsh, yet his influence remains etched in the records of scientific history.

ELEVEN

The Scientist, Philosopher and Statesman

Oppenheimer was a towering intellectual figure, whose contributions extended far beyond the realm of physics and nuclear weaponry. He was an introspective philosopher, considering the moral and philosophical implications of scientific progress, and grappling with ethical quandaries brought about by the atomic age—an era to which he significantly contributed. His philosophical reflections form an essential part of his enduring legacy.

. . .

A Scientist's Struggle with Morality

The detonation of the first atomic bomb presented Oppenheimer with a stark confrontation of the ethical consequences of his work. He famously quoted from the Bhagavad Gita, uttering, "Now I am become Death, the destroyer of worlds." This profound statement serves as a testament to the moral struggle he faced as a key architect of the atomic bomb and, consequently, mass destruction.

In subsequent years, Oppenheimer publicly wrestled with the ethical burden resting on the shoulders of the scientific community. His 'We have known sin' address to the American Philosophical Society in November 1945 underscored the moral implications of the atomic bomb. His philosophy extended beyond his personal moral dilemmas, urging scientists to consider the societal implications of their work and to engage in public policy and discourse.

Science, Society, and Responsibility

Oppenheimer's reflections were not limited to the atomic bomb. He contemplated the societal role of scientists and the intricate relationship between scientific progress and societal responsibility. The post-war world was increasingly dependent on technological and scientific advancements. In response, Oppenheimer stressed the necessity for scientists to consider the societal and ethical implications of their work.

Legacy of Thought

Decades later, Oppenheimer's philosophical and ethical musings continue to inform discussions on the ethics of scientific discovery and technological advancement. His life and work stand as a testament to the moral dilemmas scientists must face and serve as a constant reminder of the inextricable link between scientific progress and ethical responsibility.

Assessing Oppenheimer's Legacy

Oppenheimer's legacy, as a physicist, statesman of science, and philosophical thinker, is far-reaching and complex. His contribution to theoretical physics, mentoring the next generation of scientists, and his central role in one of the 20th century's defining moments - the atomic age, mark his significant influence on science, history, and society.

Remembering Oppenheimer Today

Today, Oppenheimer is remembered as a complex figure of significant brilliance and profound introspection. His story serves as a lesson in the power and peril of scientific knowledge, the inherent ethical challenges in progress, and the profound impact one individual can have on the world.

Oppenheimer's legacy prompts us to grapple with difficult questions concerning the role of science in society, the responsibility of those with knowledge, and the ethical dilemmas arising from technological advancement. His life story is a powerful narrative that continues to resonate in the 21st century, offering invaluable lessons as we navigate our era of rapid scientific and technological change. His legacy is a testament to the triumphs, dilemmas, and tragedies of the atomic age and continues to provide invaluable insight as we grapple with the moral implications of scientific and technological progress.

TWELVE

Resolving Oppenheimer's Paradox

Arriving at the conclusion of our comprehensive study of Oppenheimer's life and accomplishments, we stand before a towering figure of multifaceted complexity. As we grapple with Oppenheimer's paradox – the co-existence of his scientific brilliance and personal contradictions - we must recognize his influence as a scientist, an intellectual, and a figure of political significance. His narrative, imbued with a mosaic of achievements, challenges, and enigmas, provides a thought-provoking lens through which to view the complexities of human character, scientific progress, and historical interpretation.

A Reflection on Oppenheimer's Dualities

A quintessential aspect of understanding Oppenheimer lies in acknowledging his innate dualities, which were an integral part of his personality and scientific endeavors. Known for his formidable intellect, he often found himself grappling with personal issues, oscillating between periods of exceptional clarity and depression. He was a captivating figure capable of inspiring a team of world-class scientists, despite his reserved nature, often perceived as aloofness.

The essence of Oppenheimer is also a testament to his broad interests. This man, who was deeply embedded in the world of science, found solace and inspiration in literature and philosophy. He had an uncanny ability to bridge these seemingly disparate worlds, which in turn contributed to his unique worldview.

The dualities in Oppenheimer's scientific achievements were equally striking. While his role in the Manhattan Project resulted in the creation of an incredibly destructive force, his extensive research greatly contributed to our understanding of nuclear physics and quantum mechanics. His work exemplifies the paradox of scientific discovery - it holds the potential to both create and destroy, illuminate and obfuscate.

The Ripple Effect: Consequences of Oppenheimer's Legacy

Oppenheimer's role in the development of the atomic bomb and the ushering in of the nuclear era had far-reaching implications that extended beyond his lifetime. The paradox here lies in the duality of his legacy: the destructive power he facilitated and his advocacy for control over nuclear weapons and peaceful use of atomic energy.

The first wartime use of atomic bombs in Hiroshima and Nagasaki in 1945, with Oppenheimer at the helm of their creation, irrevocably changed the course of warfare and international politics. This era was marked by a continuous dread of nuclear weapons, sparking a significant arms race and the Cold War, which further heightened global instability.

Yet, Oppenheimer's legacy isn't confined to these momentous events. He stood as a vocal critic of the very force he helped unleash. Reflecting on the destructive power of the atomic bomb, he famously quoted the Bhagavad Gita, saying, "Now I am become Death, the destroyer of worlds," symbolizing his deep remorse and highlighting his moral conflict.

Post-war, Oppenheimer found himself embroiled in controversies and suspicion, primarily driven by his political leanings. Accusations of his communist affiliations, although unproven, resulted in his security clearance being revoked in 1954. However, even amidst this personal turmoil, his pleas for nuclear disarmament and cautionary messages about the risks of nuclear proliferation remain of profound relevance in our world today.

A Critical Examination: Controversies and Interpretations

Our exploration of Oppenheimer's paradox would be incomplete without acknowledging the diverse perspectives and criticisms that accompany his legacy. A key challenge in fully understanding Oppenheimer is the lack of comprehensive self-disclosures. Despite his prolific scientific writings, personal reflections on his ethical dilemmas and motivations are notably sparse.

Several critics also point to his alleged political affiliations, which continue to cast a shadow over his legacy. Did his political beliefs align with the American values of his time, or did he harbor sympathies towards communism during the peak of the Cold War? This question remains a point of debate and continues to fuel intrigue around his character.

Furthermore, his leadership role in the Manhattan Project has been a focal point of ethical discussions.

Did Oppenheimer fully comprehend the destructive capacity of the atomic bomb during its creation? And if so, what does it reveal about his moral judgment? These unresolved questions highlight the intricacies and ambiguities surrounding Oppenheimer and his work.

Oppenheimer's Paradox: Lessons and Reflections

As we reflect on Oppenheimer's life and work, a number of significant lessons emerge. His persistent intellectual curiosity, despite the devastating implications of his work, serves as a testament to the transformative power of knowledge. From physics to philosophy and languages, his passion for learning serves as an inspiration for scholars, students, and life-long learners.

Oppenheimer's journey also illuminates the complex nature of scientific progress. While his work led to the development of a devastating weapon, it also opened up new pathways in nuclear physics, leading to advancements in various fields. This dual nature of his scientific contributions stands as a reminder of the need for ethical deliberation in our pursuit of scientific and technological advancement.

Moreover, his transformation from the 'father of the atomic bomb' to an advocate for nuclear disarmament underscores the importance of moral courage and introspection. Even when faced with the horrifying implications of his work, Oppenheimer demonstrated a willingness to accept his mistakes and advocate for change.

Lastly, his personal trials during the height of the Cold War serve as a cautionary tale about the dangers of fear and paranoia, especially during politically sensitive periods. As the world navigates increasingly divisive and contentious times, his story underlines the importance of understanding, empathy, and constructive dialogue.

Final Thoughts: Embracing the Lessons from Oppenheimer's Paradox

As we conclude our study of Julius Robert Oppenheimer's fascinating life, we are left with a rich tapestry of insights. His life is a prism through which we can reflect on the complexities of scientific progress, historical interpretation, and human nature. His story urges us to approach scientific discovery with ethical responsibility, to learn from our past, and to promote understanding in our interactions with others.

We hope that this exploration of Oppenheimer's paradox serves not just as a historical investigation, but also as a catalyst for critical thought and conversation. As we continue to grapple with the repercussions of the Atomic Age, let us remember Oppenheimer's cautionary words and strive to balance our pursuit of scientific discovery with our ethical responsibilities towards humanity.